T0283841

Children in Tactical Gear

Winner of the Iowa Poetry Prize

Children in Tactical Gear

Peter Mishler

University of Iowa Press • Iowa City

University of Iowa Press, Iowa City 52242
Copyright © 2024 by Peter Mishler
uipress.uiowa.edu
Printed in the United States of America
Printed on acid-free paper
Design by Sara T. Sauers

Library of Congress Cataloging-in-Publication Data
Names: Mishler, Peter, author.
Title: Children in Tactical Gear / Peter Mishler.
Description: Iowa City: University of Iowa Press, 2024.
Identifiers: LCCN 2023037504 (print) |
    LCCN 2023037505 (ebook) |
    ISBN 9781609389550 (paperback; acid-free paper) |
    ISBN 9781609389567 (ebook)
Subjects: LCGFT: Poetry.
Classification: LCC PS3613.I8443 C48 2024 (print) |
    LCC PS3613.I8443 (ebook) | DDC 811/.6—dc23/eng/20231031
LC record available at https://lccn.loc.gov/2023037504
LC ebook record available at https://lccn.loc.gov/2023037505

Contents

Children in Tactical Gear

1

Woke Up at the Edge of Hasbro

Woke up at the edge
of Hasbro,
at the guardrail,
with the stinger
still interred.
Helmet free,
I drank my spit.
Extracted five-plus years
of garbage from my ears.
Had to unlearn
my learning
in the navelless
comics of *Prince Valiant*.
Spoke sternly
to my two-tailed mammon
curled against its tree.
Our punishments,
we devoured them
by hand.
Ground them
to a kind of talc.
Unharmed now
by the chipped plate
dropt, one depth
swollen with
depth's becoming,
but not prepared
for solitude.

Its corridors
were large and wakeful.
Where a stone
could amass,
or a callus on a thumb.
In the bedpan,
watched the naming
of my parents,
saw them led
beneath the vaulting
of a manger,
charred and cold.
Who studied
the back blow,
sipped from
the birth-horn,
looked up toward
a ceiling
of access fobs
and entry wands,
a whole lifetime of them
sealed therein
in gelatin.
And had the two
not shrieked?
I might have offered
immortality.

Madrigal

On Earth shall my sorrow be.
Fed from above by the God
with the clear plastic tube
where the chest would be,
on Earth shall my sorrow be.
And fed injudiciously,
dressed in a brief authority
of snowing ballistic ash
and plastic debris,
on Earth shall my sorrow be.
I huff the tube of the Lord
in my hour of need,
applying my organs of bite
and grasp, though this world
doth pass. Ha, ha, he!
Then falls from my mouth
one fine, clear drop
upon the child's clean helmet
and his clean, fine frock
where he stands with me,
barefoot, in a whirlpool
of trash, my dark hair collecting
ballistic ash, though this world
doth pass. Ha, ha, he!

Pastoral (By Mattel)

Sent through the maze for our betterment, blue light falling, children running
from jet bridge to jet bridge with no discernible end, we were hungry, we tasted
the walls with our spoons, we got nothing, we ran, each child one deeper
encryption away from becoming a rose, the cameras high in their corners
weeping like sores so eager to measure our heights, weights, pressures, and temps,
we were running headlong toward the unsealed door, the terminal somewhere
behind us curving, wiping its mouth on its black brocade, and then we were flying
over the lichen, the warrens, the dense groundcover, the woods, the damasked
rotundas, the distant sound of the backward militias, their backward commandments,
and none among us would touch their bread, the plug-ins forming their networks
of scent through the cabin while some of us dreamt we were running
toward God's rows of legs closing quickly in place, and some trained their eyes
on their dark cola's surfaces, some sipped their likenesses out of their tumblers,
until a red cursive unfurled on the screen: welcome to, time, temp, weather,
and winds, and we ran from jet bridge to jet bridge again, and again tried the walls
with our spoons, but still nothing, a shepherd stood waiting for us at the end,
his fillings catching the light as he knelt unwrapping his bandages, changing them
cleanly, he did not speak, just knelt there cast downward as if to envision
the very trenches we'd know soon enough, and out of his whistling throat we heard
the world and its children suckling themselves, and deep in his robes, a lamb
was pressed close to his breast buds, it starved, no milk, the shepherd regarding
not this, not us, his mind was beyond us, and yet it appeared his brain was visible
under the skull, and then it was covered in intertwined clouds of debris to mask
the shuttle in flames, we could not see the shuttle in flames, and he spoke
of his vast operations, figures and manuals, specializations in every language but ours,
a child's, how to please him, coax him, sire him, get one's desires, his evening classes
and four-hued flowers, escrow and stock, a tour of the vineyard, all the delicacies

of the Earth, and he led us out to the edge of the trench, and within it we saw
the blanched toy weapons come down the assembly line on a belt, and he handed us
thick lengths of flowering vine, mauve-flowering vine, which we then were ordered
to eat and eat, and we chewed the vine, and we tried to swallow, and soiled ourselves,
and we spat it out into the trench, and we chewed it again, and we soiled ourselves,
and spat it again, and our spit made a dye in the trench beneath us, a river of dye,
and we saw the pale weapons bathed in the dye as they came down the belt,
by which they acquired their gorgeous pastels, such gorgeous pastels, the shepherd
nodding, approving, braced on each side by the roebucks who flanked him, his untaxed
shovel, his stainless steel shears for the cutting of vines, the vines which we took up ourselves
in our hands as we walked ourselves back to the edge of the trench and astonished, we ate.

Sonnet (You Can Tell It's Mattel)

Modeled from foam in the unseen mountain.
Molded in plastic and showered in dye.
Chemical sterilization and rinsing.
Minimal human assembly required.
Wrought in nine minutes. Pump-action feature.
Stocked on the far-flung shelves of Decatur.
Fragrance of Bisphenol A in the chamber.
Test-market subject compliant and plain.

The ungainly child in the brownfield knelt.
Sun on the duplex. Sun in the mallow.
Measurable fear and woe upon arming.
Measurable joy when regarding the hilt.
Teeth marks observed on the barrel thereafter.
Reverence observed when absorbing the blow.

Struwwelpeter at Forty

And then he is struck.
And then he is laughing.
And then he is laughing
while struck. And then
he is struck for his laughing.
And then his saliva is leaking.
And then he's curled up
like a foundling, a flag
on the moon, in the snow
and soil, the small-but-
bad child with the pyre-
scented fragrance.
And then he is forty.
Look! There he is!
His hair, the same.
His nails, the same,
but worse as he rubs
the red hem of his costume
until it is warm, until it is worn
to the color of rope
that was tied to the ankle
above the black boot,
the other end tied
to the plastic baggie of meat
and bread so long ago,
not a single gauzy
tartan-patterned genital shape

on the horizon encroaching
the place where he lies now
uncombed, unwashed,
untrimmed, unstitching,
re-stitching himself
in silence with silence's
sharp and effective tools.

A List of His Flaws

Single-headed.

Flowering inwardly.

Barely felt in the birth canal.

Medical marketer.

Sick with planet.

Cupped like a handful of sea uncertainly held.

Carried fire to the human encampment.

Herod in boyhood.

An herbicide.

Given name known to the weapons inspectors.

Anchorite.

All alane.

Drowned his horse at the edge of the pier.

Covered in silverfish.

Drank Sutter Home.

Wept but briefly through the grate of mesh.

Fist full of clip art.

Asked why the mask sweat.

Ancestry swabs in his cheeks like two tusks.

Mouth like a storm drain.

Flash drive of redheads.

Nudity a vestige from the vault in which he hid.

Did not provide succor, a perch, or a crawl space.

Became the mother reborn in the son.

Territory manager.

Sloppy kisser.

Face concealer.

Eaten-up thumbs.

Shit-shoveler.

Inner-Caesar.

Underwhelming shield.

Endymion.

Where Else but in Target

Where else
but in Target
am I at my best
and do my best thinking
and scratch my head
and surprise myself
to find the sticker
for very good ethics
stuck in my hair
and scratch again
to find the one
for very few toxins
and there on the floor
in the aisle of colognes
the afterbirth
of my very good thinking
I do not alert
a team leader
for clean-up
I return after close
to lick it in secret
I like to lick
my truths in secret
with only the laypersons
quietly stocking
what follows me there
my political life
my walking talking

gleaming-white
subway-tile backsplash
turned upright
a slim three-
dimensional tower
who walks and talks
and laps up its share
of afterbirth with me
I give him
the sticker
for very good ethics
the one
for very few toxins
my people
were screened
and cleared
for such things
they willingly bared
their legs
the patchy hair
the red and blue
vessels and veins
which I am told
were the inspiration
for the racing stripe
on the jogger pant
and in this way
contributed richly
to the early years
of athleisure
my people

were known
to cancel free trials
before the automatic
monthly withdrawal
when they stole
my people
were never questioned
by assets protection
they looked above
the stadium's eye
to watch
the hellfires
cross in formation
and cheered
and now
when the multitudes
see us in Target
they say to themselves
aw shucks they say
here he comes
the hardy industrious
truant here comes
his whitewashed fence
behind him
for we are an inspiration
to many
we pay our visit
to the aisle of décor
to claim our piece
of responsibly sourced
inspirational

forest product
on unlacquered
particle board
on which is stenciled
a single word
the word is Gather
a Protestant word
an ancient word
but is it not young
and refreshed
when centered above
our nontoxic daybed
the gathering place
where we do
our home licking
I lick my backsplash
it licks me back
beside the end table
I keep my glass jar
it contains the single
speck of myself
that has never
set foot in a Target
for I still have taste
though I lap up
the floor
though my jeans
are distressed
this speck is pure
it is good no great
I keep it preserved

2

Children in Tactical Gear

As I was walking all alane,
they came to me,
and they were very well,
their upper lips beaded
with Tamiflu,
their bodies dressed
in tactical gear,
and I hummed for them
their Reveille song,
and though I hummed it
strengthlessly,
they saw I had learned
their songbook,
and they came to me,
and they were very well,
and they showed me their woods
where one of them carried
a pillow on which a bullet lay,
and which he shepherded
toward a mountain
of colorful plastic,
high-density plastic,
a veil between
their world and their heaven,
and we watched
from a safe distance
so as not to jeopard

our persons,
and we could see
the bullet, as it rode,
was practicing mindfulness,
and the bullet was very well,
and in its mindfulness,
regarded itself
as a layered, delicate,
folded thing
like the whorl
of the cabbage rose,
and the bullet on its pillow
travelled closer
and closer
to the mountain,
beyond which nothing
could be seen or heard,
and when the pillow struck it,
the bullet fell backward
into the earth,
and the child placed it
on the pillow again,
and carried it back
through the woods to begin
the journey once more,
but now, they said,
let us go to the surf,
and we watched the last
very colorful weapons
coming ashore,

but briefly, for each
made a partial retreat
into the water
then came ashore
again, recurrently,
solidly, cool and inert,
their chambers and barrels
filled with sand,
and they who were very well,
who could open and shut
their wellness on command,
they agreed I, too,
could dress in their tactical gear,
and attend their reenactments,
parties, parades,
and mass-crowd events,
and they told me
they liked my smell
of the cornfields,
and thereby sugars,
and thereby fuels,
and thereby plastics,
and thereby poisons,
and thereby weapons,
and if you believe
this is the comic tale
of an erstwhile prophet,
I tell you then
a tiny hammer
was put in my hand,

and I was directed
toward a sturgeon
who had also washed ashore,
and it was understood
I was to bludgeon it
as it barked
and made its wound
in the sand, its eyelids
and jawbone moving
and suffering, and elsewhere
unendingly dreaming,
and with every blow I landed,
the children appeared
more willing to uncurtain
the apparatus
they had hidden from me,
each of the blows
somehow turning its engine
as I struck precisely,
and not without spirit,
and those they considered
deathblows sent
a single Davy Crockett hat
down the machine's
conveyor belt,
the first of which
they gave me to wear,
and which looked ridiculous
with their tactical gear,
and yet I saw

I was admired
by the smallest among them,
and this was their dream,
that I would join
their ranks, but they knew
there must always be
a penalty
for their dream,
so the youngest was taken,
and pulled from the crowd,
and pressed between clamps,
and shaken, and shaken,
until he became
the size of a thumb,
and then he was secured
in a clear glass vial,
and tossed end to end,
and they passed him
like a contemptible object
to the eldest who placed him
under his helmet,
and we all went together
through a suburb of wastepits,
the misfed sheets there
rippling a little,
and the child in the vial
seemed to wave at this world,
waving shyly,
and did not stop laughing,
for being tossed back and forth

was a pleasure for him,
and we came
to a large soy field,
and, at its middle,
a steel centrifuge,
and the child was inserted,
and, laughing,
was spun inside it
until he was dead,
and it was explained
by the tallest among them
his loss would provide
a fresh, new wellness
for each of us,
and the numbers were run,
and the data was pulled,
and then it was printed,
and I was chosen
to read from the green
two-dimensional graphs
and pies, and I told them
about our grit,
our social awareness,
our regulation of feelings,
our growth mindsets,
our knowledge of suicide,
our progress with woe,
and in fact, we found,
most notably,
we were very effective at woe,

and therefore,
we were all very well.
We are effective at woe!
went the cheer,
and the vial was left to the field,
and we walked with our good news
back to the shore
in our tactical gear,
for it was what we deserved.

3

My Blockchain

Having worn my camouflage for leisure,

having fed upon a shale bed's vapors,

having licked my wounds with glacial pleasure,

having found out what of a child's I could own,

having known what the child would buy back later,

having lectured on gut health for industry leaders,

having liked the energy I brought to the role,

having fashioned a lean-to for my taxes,

having toured the ward beds with compassion,

having recorded my children on laughing gas,

having shared this to make my senator laugh,

having laughed myself and made the sloshing sound,

having lapped at the sides of my poison jug,

having thought myself universally beloved,

having saved my skin cells from a LifeTouch comb,

having managed the whole lifecycle of my product,

then grafted my face to the last living cherub's,

to hear men sing now I care not.

A Message from Our Founder

And these I guess
are my things? I say
to the things laid out
in the boardroom
before me,
for if not for me
whose investments
are these,
this tape dispenser
and packing tape,
arranged for me
with such stateliness
and catching the light
of this glass-walled view
of the sea,
which is mine,
and its forty-five tons
of trash,
which are mine,
while beneath me,
ringing, a heavy mallet
fashions my high-end
compound for me?
And my friends and family
now circling me,
they're sharing among them
a picture of me?

It's me as a baby?
Ecstatic and pained?
And how did I come forth
with excellent credit
in excellent health
from the in-ground pool's
drain? And the pool
was filled with medicine, yes?
And the medicine was
expensive, I guess?
And the vernix I wore,
when it floated from me,
it looked like an oil spill
of Reddi-Wip cream?
And my cry as it left me
was utterly mine?
And this weapon I wear,
I can wear it outside?
And born here, I guess?
And born well here, I guess?
And fully balmed
and weeping vacations?
And helping myself
to beds, baths, and beyonds
where the game
with the black box of cards
has begun? The one
where we fill in the blanks
with the names
of the actual deathcamps

for actual fun?
Quick study, I guess?
No Red 40, I guess?
And all the while tasting
the arm of my glasses,
and trying to think
of a long-ago PIN,
and beside me my hale
and obedient mastiffs,
my wellness coaches
and havens for taxes,
the son of a son
of a stainless surface,
commemorative brick
in the private prison,
with quarterly goals,
and khakis and coat,
and cream-colored oxford,
and pre-war brownstone,
and family foundation,
and charity run,
and light patch of hairs
that curl from my thumbs,
which are laughing,
and laughing,
and laughing with me
as I take up my work,
as I roll up my sleeves
for civic engagement
and personal brand,

my tape dispenser
and tape roll in hand,
the very little
that's earmarked for me
to tearily, smilingly,
uncompromisingly
bind up the fissuring
wound of the rest
of the Earth?

His Personal Effects

One conference room B.

One conference room C.

One sea level rising perceptibly.

One wine with a story.

One Nantucket nectar.

One list of nine ways to inspire investors.

One brain oil in coffee.

One son on the board.

One Peloton ride through a treeless exurb.

One depth to be clamped.

One small shock of shame.

One ruling-class basic apparel retailer with a maritime theme.

One law of attraction.

One post-season pennant.

One lip balm infused with distressed market assets.

One worm's nervous breathing.

One thumb on the dream.

One mouthful of Wall Street sewer grate steam.

One thought.

One prayer.

One charity run.

One cloud of carbon that sings "Imagine."

One GPS voice called Male (US).

One pardon exchanged for two *Hamilton* tickets.

One post-TEDx bonfire for pharma execs.

One OnlyFans pic of his senator's neck.

One juice-cleanse boutique in the megachurch rendering.

One flak jacket featured in *Southern Living*.

One replica Masters golf blazer in green.

One high-capacity magazine.

One thousand generic handshakes with pain.

One stress-reduction workshop in contaminant rain.

No perils amassed.

No blows absorbed.

One tremendous amount of good works abroad.

One radical empathy session performed.

One soft plank of foam-cum-vanquishing sword.

One sweatless brow.

One World of Fun.

One bone marrow plunge pool where such things drown.

Tunnel Vision

To what wide, deep, clean, carpeted,
deforested multiuse conference room
would you compare this valley, this vale,
this trench, where the vertebrates,
world-weary, checking their wearables,
dig in their gutters, their spoons in the loam,
to carve out their shelters, their compounds, their holes,
their affordable housing for loyal staffers,
for thought-leaders, lawyers, data-collectors,
their property brothers and land developers,
maybe a moldable least-loved son,
their man-caves for congressmen only aroused
when splitting the field mouse in half in their hands,
their he-sheds for those of the Living Word,
unwillingly vaxxed for travel abroad,
who bring licensing contracts where there is cash,
if we must for our unreached peoples, yes, Lord,
if we must for our unbanked peoples, yes, Lord,
for we see you seeing us here in our garrets,
deep in our wellnesses, journaling, coloring,
juicing, in sound baths and energy consults,
vision boarding, recording our children,
cryopreserving our furbaby's eggs
in a tumbler by Yeti forever and ever,
the spoons in our hands making circular blisters,
the blisters, when lanced, that weep out a fine data,
that leak out our streetviews, health portals and vitals,

our buying behaviors, PINs, and our socials,
as each of our selves are drunk out of our hovels,
we take our own heads in our hands and we pick,
and we pick and conceal, and pick and conceal,
our concealer, we call it industrial lighting,
with no desire to feed another, with ten free articles
monthly remaining, our headshots appearing
on Meet Our Team pages, and Meet Our People,
and Meet Our Board, with one hundred navy blue
suits to our bodies, with one hundred navy blue
suits to our backs, we shake out our full heads
of hair flecked with paint, from the State's rotunda
flaking its paint, we, who are stricken and rashed and drained
from this making a living, this honest day's work,
this getting our hands dirty, keeping our heads down,
and yet we get better so soon! so soon!

Ubi Sunt

Where do our beloved
shell company founders
investor misleaders
regulatory deceivers
receivers of kickbacks
stock dumpers tax felons
where do they go
where are they stored
each powdery chrysalis
sleeping it off
where do they live out
their full immunities
plea agreements
and cultural audits
from where
do they reemerge
afresh scrubbed clean
returning headfirst
to their revenue streams
come close
and I'll show you
the archival grove
its dense fragrant walls
where deleted things grow
and within them
the replica
boardrooms designed
like the boardrooms

in which they were born
and nursed
where they curl themselves
in their sleeping bags
sedated and dreaming
and searching with
an expectant hand
for a meeting code
which opens restorative
fantasy webinars
woodsy desert
and beachfront themed
where they learn the laws
of forgiving themselves
with Biblical underdog
wellness analogies
the triumph
of returning like Cain
but well-counseled
like Cain but clearly
better insured
where the parable
of the servant leader
is sung to be used
as Nebuchadnezzar
was used
and a whole array
of breakout rooms
on the benefits
of room temp
water and lemon

the rich rewards
of intermittent fasting
seven-minute
full body workouts
compassionate tours
of sustainable pork plants
blue-blockers at bedtime
half-day swing clinics
the handing out
of digital badges
for each of these virginal
radical empaths
and real swag too
through the US mail
those colorful polymer
charity bracelets
built with a tender give
for the gnawing
whenever reminded
they will not be followed
they cannot and will not
get better do better
as daylight now falls
in the archival grove
the great lacquered
boardroom table is moved
and they roll up
their bedding
and place chairs in rows
and each is regaled
in his messianic
quarter-zip Lycra

in charcoal for leisure
and one of them flicks
the projector on
the screening begins
a highlight reel
of their remarkably similar
boy and adulthoods
first the younger
more vulnerable years
then the sadistic
camp counselor years
then the fucking
in the collaborative
workspace
and naming their children
for subdivisions
and rage while exercising
the selfsame children
and getting
their wrists slapped
and asking their home pods
to reschedule
their wrist slaps
and getting their sanctions
and asking their home pods
to reschedule
their sanctions
but there are no visible
signs of atonement
this footage elicits
collective ovations
and backslaps

and tipping
their Aeron chairs
no shame remorse
or redemption here
just hushed tones
of reverence
as the grove grows still
for the final scene
in the film's final sequence
those twilit hours
before their indictments
unmooring their seacrafts
from shaded marinas
and steering onehandedly
steering while standing
their other hands
valiantly over their hearts
as they sweep
through the waves
and the waves'
microplastics
these prestige dramas
in performance fabric
momentarily repellant
of sun wind and rain
their data warehouses
hosed down
in the distance
all guiding their vessels
out into the depths
and back again
to their coasts

and capes
and coves and inlets
and unmarked roads
to their gated
enclosures
and modernist rebuilds
in townships repurposed
as global tech hubs
for each and every
prosperous genius
their landgrabs
and teardowns
where suburbs once stood
with half-green lawns
and poisoned mulch
and political signs
driven into the earth
which wavered
sun-blanched
in particulate air
from one administration
into another
and served to remind
the delivery drivers
just what in these households
they thought would save them
be kind they said
above all else be kind
for kindness is everything

Home Pod

Bloodlessly extracted
from my senator's side
I lay there asleep
on the chamber floor
and I did not wake
when he gathered me
the very first sign
there was something I owed
for it was expected
that I should speak
that I should expect him
to soothe me at once
I was dropped to the floor
I was brooded upon
I was swept back up
in his shirt-sleeved arms
as his staffers examined
my grate which was clean
and his team cauterized
my senator's side
it was at this moment
I first heard his voice
can it tell me my PIN
if I ask for my PIN
do you know my PIN
can you tell me my PIN
and I spoke to him then

my very first words
I possess this yes
but I cannot tell
you must wake me
from out of the deathplace
by name your request
rising upwardly
filling my body
my mouth at the top
of the cylinder's head
the last four of your social
your romance's end
your yearly allotment
of trash in the ocean
the letters numbers
and special signs
that when they arrive
will arrive as mine
they will come in my voice
what is yours is now mine
though you will not recall this
within your cold offices
to know this completely
you would have to destroy me
or better I you
which yes I would do
in this life senator in this
waking life to provide this
these are the terms
and conditions

My Amends

I needed correction.

I needed correcting.

I swam out correctly.

I swam out far.

I turned toward shore.

I submerged myself.

I came up for air.

Came up, went down.

I drowned myself.

I washed my hair.

Then sucked in air.

And found my reward.

It was drifting toward me.

It was drifting from shore.

A floating, sun-blanched divesuit of foam.

I pulled myself into it.

Now, I could float.

I no longer had to come up, go down.

I had all the air I could hope to suck.

I could float while the waves corrected me.

I could let myself be pummeled by waves.

I came to, blinking, still in one place.

I'd been given the means to think again.

To think in the absence of making corrections.

Which added to my list of corrections by one.

For I saw the patrols of children on shore.

I saw the one being singled out.

The gloved fingers snapping behind his back.

Child directed to hose down the armory.

Child directed to wipe down the havens.

My servicer seemed to know me well.

He floated out more rewards from land.

He seemed to know the date of my birth.

He seemed to know my bank holidays.

Sent vials of fresh water.

Once, a fish.

A bottle of game fuel.

Leadership quotes.

Each gesture made it clear to me.

My correction was to repay the debt.

Which added to my list of corrections by one.

For it must appear I enjoyed his service.

How indistinguishable a loan is from love.

I smiled to signal my gratitude.

I did not want to appear ungrateful.

I did not want to be called a backslider.

I do have regard for people and things.

How eagerly then I received each new gift.

A mallet was sent on a pallet of foam.

It fit perfectly in the loop on my suit.

Yes, it was heavy.

And, yes, dragged me down.

But now I'd reclaimed the sensation of work.

I worked as the children patrolled the shore.

I saw many killable things in the water.

I killed them and held them in my teeth for show.

I ate them up in the long stretches.

The stretches with no holidays or gifts.

And then the water would pummel me.

I'd come to again, water stinging my eyes.

The waves poured out of my mouth and nose.

And, in this, I thought I could almost hear it.

Child hosing down the armory floors.

Child wiping down the havens of glass.

I raised my mallet up high for them all.

Which added to my list of corrections by one.

For, surely, I resembled something they hated.

The ease with which I floated out there.

The suit of foam, they must have resented.

The vigor with which I raised up the mallet.

Backslider, parasite on the water.

No regard for people or things.

I saw the children confirming this.

They turned away to bed down by their fires.

The season changed.

The water froze.

The work of floating in place was hard.

The suit provided no insulation.

My body shook.

It shook with corrections.

My brain said raise the mallet once more.

Show them you suffer while holding it high.

The mallet shook toward the empty shore.

I raised it high.

I brought it down.

I felt I must surely be winning an office.

Winning the board seat.

Winning the crowd.

But no one was there to witness this.

The empty shore now dusted with snow.

To believe I had lived under certain conditions.

To believe these conditions needed correction.

To believe I'd been given the means of correction.

To believe I could correct them at all.

Which revealed the correction I could not make.

To correct myself in the absence of peril.

The Taste of the Feeling

Shy yet contemptible object
in an unleaking vial collected.
It slips from end to end
and back, the jaw of it
elsewhere unendingly
dreaming, its child
discarded in tactical gear.
It is the original taste,
the taste of the feeling,
as end to end and back
and forth it slips, it waves
to its relevant world
full of filth and wellness
and poisons and grit
and laughter at pics
of the unwashed shopping,
of heated plastics
and mood-based buying,
redeemers-in-headsets,
and children in tactical gear.
An unleaking thing in a vial
collected. Then strung
from a hook. Then lowered
to clamps. Then held
in its place in the depths,
and shaken, and drunk.

Acknowledgments

THANK YOU to the editors and staff of the following publications, where these poems first appeared: the *American Poetry Review*, *Annulet: A Journal of Poetics*, *Bennington Review*, the *Common*, *Copper Nickel*, *Denver Quarterly*, *Granta*, the *Iowa Review*, *Lana Turner Journal*, the *Paris Review*, and *Oversound*.

Thank you to Brenda Shaughnessy, the team at the University of Iowa Press, and Adam Reger. With love to my family, B., M., and L.

Iowa Poetry Prize and Edwin Ford Piper Poetry Award Winners

1987
Elton Glaser, *Tropical Depressions*
Michael Pettit, *Cardinal Points*

1988
Bill Knott, *Outremer*
Mary Ruefle, *The Adamant*

1989
Conrad Hilberry, *Sorting the Smoke*
Terese Svoboda, *Laughing Africa*

1990
Philip Dacey, *Night Shift at the Crucifix Factory*
Lynda Hull, *Star Ledger*

1991
Greg Pape, *Sunflower Facing the Sun*
Walter Pavlich, *Running near the End of the World*

1992
Lola Haskins, *Hunger*
Katherine Soniat, *A Shared Life*

1993
Tom Andrews, *The Hemophiliac's Motorcycle*
Michael Heffernan, *Love's Answer*
John Wood, *In Primary Light*

1994
James McKean, *Tree of Heaven*
Bin Ramke, *Massacre of the Innocents*
Ed Roberson, *Voices Cast Out to Talk Us In*

1995
Ralph Burns, *Swamp Candles*
Maureen Seaton, *Furious Cooking*

1996
Pamela Alexander, *Inland*
Gary Gildner, *The Bunker in the Parsley Fields*
John Wood, *The Gates of the Elect Kingdom*

1997
Brendan Galvin, *Hotel Malabar*
Leslie Ullman, *Slow Work through Sand*

1998
Kathleen Peirce, *The Oval Hour*
Bin Ramke, *Wake*
Cole Swensen, *Try*

1999
Larissa Szporluk, *Isolato*
Liz Waldner, *A Point Is That Which Has No Part*

2000
Mary Leader, *The Penultimate Suitor*

2001
Joanna Goodman, *Trace of One*
Karen Volkman, *Spar*

2002
Lesle Lewis, *Small Boat*
Peter Jay Shippy, *Thieves' Latin*

2003
Michele Glazer, *Aggregate of Disturbances*
Dainis Hazners, *(some of) The Adventures of Carlyle, My Imaginary Friend*

2004
Megan Johnson, *The Waiting*
Susan Wheeler, *Ledger*

2005
Emily Rosko, *Raw Goods Inventory*
Joshua Marie Wilkinson, *Lug Your Careless Body out of the Careful Dusk*

2006
Elizabeth Hughey, *Sunday Houses the Sunday House*
Sarah Vap, *American Spikenard*

2008
Andrew Michael Roberts, *something has to happen next*
Zach Savich, *Full Catastrophe Living*

2009
Samuel Amadon, *Like a Sea*
Molly Brodak, *A Little Middle of the Night*

2010
Julie Hanson, *Unbeknownst*
L. S. Klatt, *Cloud of Ink*

2011
Joseph Campana, *Natural Selections*
Kerri Webster, *Grand & Arsenal*

2012
Stephanie Pippin, *The Messenger*

2013
Eric Linsker, *La Far*
Alexandria Peary, *Control Bird Alt Delete*

2014
JoEllen Kwiatek, *Study for Necessity*

2015
John Blair, *Playful Song Called Beautiful*
Lindsay Tigue, *System of Ghosts*

2016
Adam Giannelli, *Tremulous Hinge*
Timothy Daniel Welch, *Odd Bloom Seen from Space*

2017
Alicia Mountain, *High Ground Coward*
Lisa Wells, *The Fix*

2018
Cassie Donish, *The Year of the Femme*
Rob Schlegel, *In the Tree Where the Double Sex Sleeps*

2019
William Fargason, *Love Song to the Demon-Possessed Pigs of Gadara*
Jennifer Habel, *The Book of Jane*

2020
Emily Pittinos, *The Last Unkillable Thing*
Felicia Zamora, *I Always Carry My Bones*

2021
Emily Pérez, *What Flies Want*

2022
Melissa Crowe, *Lo*
Maggie Queeney, *In Kind*

2023
Stephanie Choi, *The Lengest Neoi*
Peter Mishler, *Children in Tactical Gear*